Spirit of the Horse:
An Equine Anthology

Featuring poems by:

Rebecca Baez, Miriam Bat-Ami, Patricia Brooks,
Marilyn Burkhardt, Hélène Cardona, Emily Cross,
Marcella Cross, Jerri Hardesty, Gwen Hart,
Jacqueline Kolosov, Matt Kraunelis, Nina E. Larsen,
Jim LaVilla-Havelin, Joan Leotta, Barbara Mackay,
Clare D. Mazur, Mary McDonough, Jordan Nichols,
Phyllis Price, DeMar Regier, Kathy Truders,
Lisa Underwood, and Mary Wlodarski

Finishing Line Press
Georgetown, Kentucky

Spirit of the Horse:
An Equine Anthology

ACKNOWLEDGMENTS

Editor: Leah Maines

Cover Art: Melora Walters

Cover Design: Elizabeth Maines

Printed in the USA on acid-free paper.
Order online: www.finishinglinepress.com
also available on amazon.com

Author inquiries and mail orders:
Finishing Line Press
P. O. Box 1626
Georgetown, Kentucky 40324
U. S. A.

Table of Contents

I am pleased to present to you the winners of this year's Horse Anthology Poetry Competition. Our first place winner is Jordan Nichols for her poem "Cigar (1990-2014)." Honorable Mentions go to 14 year-old Marcella Cross for her poem "Race Course," and 16 year-old Emily Cross for her poem "The Final Word."

In addition to our winner and Honorable Mentions, we have included over twenty authors of merit—all sharing a love of horses.

This collection includes beautiful original cover art by famed artist, poet, screenwriter, and actor Melora Walters.

It is my hope that reading these poems will bring you closer to the "spirit of the horse" that flows from here in the bluegrass and beyond.

Cheers,

Leah Maines

Cigar (1990-2014)

Standing serenely in your stall,
Do you remember the track,
The crumble of the rich dirt,
Sand and clay—freshly churned
For your hooves,
And yours alone, as you finally found your stride—
Cantering easily
Along, Floating past the others
Like the commoners they were,
Peasants before a king?
And you, Ruler of the Track,
With your muscles of iron beneath
A coat of maple and
Points of ebony,
Do you remember advancing,
Leaving the others behind,
Soaring beyond
The monuments of memory left
By your predecessors: Secretariat
And Spectacular Bid, Nashua
And Native Dancer,
Until only Citation remained?
And do you remember how his record—
Sixteen stakes, sixteen wins—
You ticked off your girth?
The world's richest races fell beneath your feet
As you circled the serfs—
An electron charged
With the power of the sun.
Do you remember the strength
And the courage, as your chief rivals—
The best they could throw against you
Succumbed to your awesome speed?
Do the cheers still ring

In your alert ears?
Does the grainy film play
In your amber eyes?
Do these fragments of glory
Play through your mind as you look
Deep into my eyes
And accept the peppermint
From my trembling hand?

Race Course

Here they come now
Their thundering hooves
Who will reach it first?
The snowy hill
The blue sky
Their manes flowing
Like a breeze
Their breath making gentle clouds in front
And their thundering hooves leaving prints in the snow
Who will win?
That one right now
But now the other is in the lead
Their wild and carefree eyes
Looking only at the end of their course
Now the first is winning again
Their fluid motion
Graceful
Running with true speed
Here they come now
Almost there
Breathing harder
With a soft gleam of sweat
Looking at nothing
Only at the prize
The apple at the end of the field

Our Own Kind

When I was twelve, my best friend and I were horse crazy.

We used to run along the drainage ditch on the outskirts of town,
pretending we were horses.

We could trot, canter, and gallop for hours
and never get tired.

One day we ran further than usual.
We came across several horses fenced in with barbed wire.

It was getting dark, and we could just see their big dark shapes
against the pale grass and grey sky.

They drifted over to the fence
and we stroked their long necks and bony faces.

On the way home, we walked slowly,
leaving them behind on their plot of tumbleweeds and dry grass.

On the edge of a vast prairie,
we had met our own kind.

The Horse

Out of nowhere, came a horse,
the white horse followed the car all the way
on the bumpy forest road.
We drove as fast as we could,
but the small, old car couldn't go faster
than a horse.
I saw the horse in the back window,
furious,
offended in some way.

I started throwing sugar cubes
out of the window:
I always carry them;
when I am grumpy, it helps.
The horse didn't care about them,
so we slowed down
worried that the horse,
would explode his heart.

The horse didn't stop,
he just continued running,
as if he had more pre-historic reasons for running
and judging from the crazy eyes,
he was very late.

Along Apple Trails

The apple tree fell one night
we recalled the mighty crack followed by the crash
disrupting dinner and all the moments spent
under the expansive branches
It had been the starting post for wagon rides
down the grassy slope of our backyard
had overseen four of us
as we learned to ride our two-wheelers
beginning our lessons near the bottom of the hill
then honing our skills until we could pilot from
her ancient trunk at the top
In fall we raked leaves and forgotten fruit
forming twisted roads to navigate,
bikes bumping along, careening nearly out of control
heart pounding thrills
accompanied by laughter

Come morning
I brought one last game to share
Across her mighty limb
I lay an old baby blue, bassinet mattress
—a perfect saddle—
ropes, one fashioned into stirrups
another attached to a branch for reins
Into that saddle I climbed
and under summer skies splashed with horse tail clouds
we rode my imagination

The Dance

In May when frost had breathed her last,
and strawberry blooms lay bridal-white
upon the vines
my father hitched himself to Bill,
tossing the reins over his shoulders
where the leather hung worn and supple.
I was too young to do much more than watch.

Mumbling words in language only Bill could understand,
my father clicked his tongue, leaned into the plow
and they began—partners so familiar they stepped and turned
in time—man and horse a synchrony of labor by design.
Before the final row, my father lifted me onto the back
of the beast. "Hang on to the harness. Talk to him a little,
he's gentle as a lamb."

Marah

That August we buried all
promise of him, my unborn child,
whose eyes never opened

And ten months later,
on the Solstice, the bay mare
arrived, the trailer pulling in
an hour shy of midnight

Bitter, bitter jewel
what do you offer…

Four swirls of light
joined just above the horse's soft, dark eyes

Days earlier she had known
the lush green of the south
now she wakes to arid land

No need to speak to her
of my dead child

This quiet being
who after rolling in the dust of afternoon
plunged into the brackish water trough

and I laughed

Postcard

My seventh grade
Best friend Bernie
Moved to Frankfort, Kentucky
Before grade eight.

I wrote, from Pittsburgh.
She did not write back.
Finally, just before Christmas,
She sent a postcard of
A lone horse in a bluegrass pasture.
A young thoroughbred.
I taped it to my bedroom wall.
Long after I forgot Bernie's
Favorite ice cream flavor,
That sleek bay colt
continued to, nightly,
jump his paddock fence
and prance into my dreams.

Ode to a Filly

My love for her is pure and wild
In her zeal she reaches my inner child.
We walk the pasture engrossed in each other
Not looking back, not searching for mother.
Since the day she was born, only three months ago
I entered her world with full acceptance, I know.

She hurt her knee and I felt such despair
She doesn't deserve this. It's not fair!
Relegated to her stall, her best friend outside
She looks at me with hope. I want to hide.
But I must do what is right. It's such a test.
She needs to be cared for. Her leg must rest.

So I pet and caress her and try to explain.
She begs, she implores, she looks with disdain.
Why can't she go out? What has she done?
Life was so great. Now it's not fun.

Her playmate trots by with a twinkle in her eye
Come on, she whinnies, lets run, lets fly.
Lets leap in the air and play tag all day
Then return hot and tired and help mom with her hay.

But she's twisted her knee and now must heal
While my guilt consumes and my senses reel.
4 to 6 weeks they say we met wait
4 to 6 weeks til we walk to the gate
4 to 6 weeks there is so much at stake
4 to 6 weeks, we will have to wait.

Meditation on Grooming

Start with the curry comb:
Rub the cheek,
roll down the neck,
around the shoulder,
over the chest,
along the front of the foreleg,
over the knee,
around the pastern.
Return to standing.

Circle over the withers,
wipe under the belly,
over the ribcage,
press over the back
over the hips and haunches,
massage the hamstring,
over the hocks,
down the back of the hind leg,
around the pastern.
Move to the other side.
Repeat.

With the soft brush:
Wisp the forehead,
trace the cheek,
glide down the neck,
around the front of the shoulder,
sweep over the chest,
down the front leg
all the way to the coronet band.
Stand.

Brush the belly in broad strokes,
flick the dust from the back,
over the hips and haunches,
past the tail,
down the back leg.
Move to the other side.
Repeat.
Repeat.
Repeat.

Counterbalance

walking in slow circles—
a slave to the pace of life
I find myself lost in the fantasy
of a different motion—
a movement towards grace and freedom
no longer ringsour
my heart, like a stallion collected
moves me to a deeper pasture
where lush meadows thrive
and the touch of the equestrienne
is all that I need to save me.

I am breaking away from the
counterbalance of life
expressing myself
in the stillness of motion
rhapsodizing in the soul's
duality and substance.

this fantasy, unlike life
soars like an extended piaffe
trotting in mid-air
yet standing still
rhyming with the breathtaking
harmony and rhythm
surrounding it.

gravity pulls back even dreams
weighing them down with honesty
yet, reality is not without whim—
so, ardently I wait
for my heart to ride
the stallion once again
into a pasture of promise, grace
and freedom.

War Mount

In broken English
old man Heinrich Preisch
agreed to give a horse
to the cause of the Revolution—
no uniform, no gun,
but service all the same
so said the Rebel Army.

The Major took her lead,
tipped his hat and headed west.
Heinrich watched until their silhouettes
were lost in the timberline
along the Shenandoah.
In the barn the mare's scent was strong,
her presence lingered.

"She's gone then?" Mary asked
over the supper table.
"Aye. Aye."
Head bowed, between spoonfuls
of steaming soup, he mumbled,
"She was a good one.
Never see another one like her."

Draft Horse Run

Silver body back lit by fiery late afternoon sun,
Arching, then stretching,
Head high, nostrils flared, eyes bright, legs churning.
Feet hit the ground, a sound like thunder rumbling,
Hooves dig into the Earth,
Spinning it beneath him as he runs up the hill.

Three gray mares charge after him,
Tails streaming, manes flickering like flames,
Solid round bodies twisting, prancing,
Impossible grace in their movements,
Dancing to the drumbeats of joyous abandon,
Of being alive on a cold winter's day.

Together. A herd. A family.

In the silence after his death,
Snow geese, with their raucous cries,
Pass far above his grave.
As they capture his spirit and wing into the starlit night,
The sound of his thunder fades in the darkness.

Rhythms

One and two and three and four and
One and two and three and four.
The hooves beneath me
Match the beating of my heart,
Or perhaps I have fallen in synch
With them
Over years of sharing rhythm.

One-two, one-two, one-two, one-two.
Pace increases to a trot.
Pulse quickens also.
It still happens,
It is still magical,
This symbiosis of man and animal,
This friendship beyond species.

One, two, three, one, two, three, one, two, three.
Easing into a lope,
As natural as a rocking chair
And just as peaceful;
The body knows this motion,
Responds to the pitch and roll
With liquid abdomen,
Fluidly conforming
To the balance of power
Suspended
Above the racing ground.

Winter Horse

What kind of a horse?
A miraculous kind of horse.
    —Steven Spielberg

I dream for a living —
glimmer at the edge of life,
a clock with many hands,
shape-shifter moving through different worlds.
I sail on the endeavor, captain musician,
not knowing whether I'm a ghost.
I take the road
to the end of the skyline.
My mother blows directions in my ear
from the other side.
The spokes of the wheel loosen
amidst thoughts like windstorms
containing all humanity.
I manifest fulfilled in the land of shadows,
resilient winter horse.

From *Life in Suspension* (Salmon Poetry, 2016)

Ode to Star

You sensed my thirteen-year old
tentativeness, the slight body
that didn't settle into the saddle,
unsure hands to handle reins.

your tempered turns, graceful gait
brought assurance
while ears pocketed plans
mane kept secrets safe

in competition
head proud, regal as
commands were flawlessly followed
blue ribbons brought home

in time I hung my saddle on a stall peg
nuzzled your neck, patted firm flanks
ran fingers through your mane
left for college

the day I brought my husband
your ears flicked back, but when I whispered
"You are coming with us,"
brown eyes danced.

Music Education

When it was our choice,
we picked the songs we found
hilarious, like "Senor Dongato,"
about a cat who faints after reading
a love letter and is revived
by the smell of fish,
or "Goodbye, Old Paint."
We thought the paint was paint
on the wall, someone crying over
old chipped paint, peeling paint, cracked
green paint like the paint we picked at
when Mr. Door wasn't looking,
pulling it off the walls in long strips
or thick chips we flung at each other,
you know, paint. This was before
Jordan's mother drove her Chevy
off a cliff on purpose, before
Cheryl's sister got cancer,
long before Kim lost
the baby and Trey skidded
across the highway
on his head. We knew sorrow
about as well as we knew
horses. We thought we would
hear it coming, hoofbeats
like thunder, not like the low,
steady rhythm of the drum
in the corner, the small one
that set the tempo
for everything
we sang.

Headfirst: A South Texas Tale

the day her horse reared
maybe at a snake's rattle
and threw her headfirst
into the cactus patch

and how much time it took
to pull each cactus spine
from her hide

as the horse stood
nervously, guiltily by

Just Like Her

Nobody knows all of Dancer's history.
Nobody knows if all the stories
are true or not.
She has a long history
of being saved:
from abuse,
from slaughter.
Some of that history is documented
in the American Quarter Horse Registry.
The fact that it is documented
means that she was worth something
to someone
at one time or another.
It's easy to see Dancer's worth.
She isn't one of those fancy modern Quarter Horses
whose legs and hooves are sometimes too thin
for their larger bodies.
Dancer is an Old Foundation QH
with strong legs and big hooves.
She was bred well and would have done well
if it weren't for somebody or other
who wanted more.
In the horse world there are a whole lot of somebodies
who want more than what they've got.
In the horse world there are a whole lot of somebodies
who want to make what they've got
into something they'll never get,
not from the horse they have.
If they knew what they had,
they'd feel a whole lot differently.
Dancer has a long and complicated history
which isn't that surprising for a horse.

What's surprising are the stories:
how she was saved from abuse;
how she was saved from slaughter: twice,
and how she has a baby somewhere
who might very well be
just like her.

Love at Last Sight

I didn't even need to saddle you up.
It was enough just to look at you grazing,
long-necked and exotic as a giraffe
nibbling rare, green grass
in the sunburned pasture.

You were a supermodel in a herd of ordinary:
platinum mane, flawless hide sleek, white and freckled,
sixteen hands tall and long-legged,
stirring clouds of thick, red dust
as you kicked up your heels.

You stuck your perfect pink nose in the air,
sniffed my scent on the breeze, and
satisfied that I posed no threat,
ignored me.

I always loved the smell of you.
Sweating, you emanated a polite horsey fragrance,
subtle as fine leather gloves and sweet as fresh-baled hay.
I'd rest my face against your neck like a pillow,
close my eyes, and breathe you in deep.

I had no daughter, so I spent hours at the barn
grooming you, brushing and braiding your blond mane
and brushing and oiling your long, dark tail
until you looked like a Disney princess.

Your kohl-rimmed eyes spoke love to a lonely heart.
You'd bat long lashes and sigh warm breath in my face
(apple and molasses)
and I'd inhale it like oxygen.
You always were a flirt,
your stall in the center of the barn,

and you the center of attention,
painted beauty in a bevy of plain brown.

You made me feel like the only one.
I'd sneak into the barn, call *hello, my love,*
and you'd poke your fine head over the door,
a whinny and a nod in reply.
("You had me at hello.")

You were as kind as you were beautiful.
Remember the time my saddle broke loose
and rolled under your belly
like a pack of hungry wolves?
I was grateful you gave me time to jump off
before you went crazy.

I'm not as brave as you.
I let my fear come between us,
afraid we couldn't afford the luxury of a horse,
afraid I was getting too old to ride,
afraid I'd get hurt, or worse.

I sold you to a very nice woman, who loves you.
She keeps you in your old stall, where you're still the star.
I reduced my risk of financial ruin and personal injury,
and got cancer instead.
It was worse than falling off a horse.

I came out to visit you the other day.
It had been so long, and I just needed to see you
in the spring sunshine.
I wanted to see if you'd remember.

I brought you a Granny Smith apple, cut up just so.

Daisies dotted the green grass carpet where you grazed,
and the sky was the color of Cinderella's dress.
You looked up, and took my breath away.
I saw your nostrils twitch.
Hello, my love, I called.
And you came,
running.

Redeemer

The look in your eye,
like an impish child
planning his next feat;

and that snort contains
an arrogant flair
like Bucephalus might make.

Still—
You never seem to fail
to touch my soul.

Walking on Air

They say it isn't possible.
To do so would be improbable.
It simply could never happen
because of Newton's gravity.

But you carry me with such levity,
a noble horse without vanity,
who gently moves across every locality
as if walking on air.

Hiring A Horse

I always request
The most unbroken one,
The horse way too wild
For others to want.
And no thank you,
No saddle,
I just want to ride
Flesh to flesh,
Sweat to sweat,
Muscle to muscle,
Arms wrapping around his neck,
Legs tight to his flanks,
Both our manes flying,
Both our hearts pounding,
My feet becoming
his hooves,
hard on dirt,
sharp on rock,
charging straight up
any height we encounter
as we gallop together,
neither fearing the other,
both entrusting our power.

Luke

there was one who always walked alone
he waited until the others left the corral
and headed toward the open plane
then he began his solitary stroll

if I met him along the way
he eloquently brushed me aside
with a shift of his head
and a lengthening of his stride

I called him Luke
and he seemed to know his name
art least he raised his head when I spoke
though I never called for him to come to me

I never tried to break or saddle him
so ranchers said I made him useless
not fit to ride, not fit to sire, useless
except for horsemeat or glue

yet when he wandered alone
a part of me
my soul perhaps
kept pace beside him

I was nourished when he nibbled
at prairie grass, refreshed
when he paused to drink
from a nearby creek

and when he was dying
he let me sit by his side

The Last Word

You can never get the last word in
With a horse.
Especially not, when
You are standing at her stall
Guiltily telling that horse
That you can't, in fact, ride her today
And try to placate her with an apple.
But she finally convinces you
That your teachers and homework come first
Only after her.
You can never get the last word in
With a horse.
Especially not, when
You are saddling that horse up
And you forget to tighten the girth strap
After which, you get on and slide halfway around
And have to get off and try again
But she stubbornly holds her breath
Then whickers and you know that
She's laughing at you.
You can never get the last word in
With a horse.
Especially not, when
You are lying on your back
Staring up at that horse
And noticing the saddle
You recently vacated
And the expression on that horse's face
Telling you so clearly that
I told you so.
You can never get the last word in
With a horse.

First Place Winner!

Jordan Nichols is a junior studying English, Spanish, and Equine Studies at South Dakota State University in Brookings, South Dakota. Ever since she was a little girl, animals have been her passion. From her childhood days of taming wild frogs and garter snakes to her young adulthood of volunteering at the Brookings Humane Society, she has adored every member, no matter how seemingly insignificant, of the animal kingdom. But horses have always been her greatest love. As a 10-year-old, Jordan was introduced to this magnificent species at a local riding class. The next decade was spent devouring every book on horses she could reach, studying the history of thoroughbred racing, and, of course, riding every chance she could. Jordan's love reached a pinnacle during the spring break of her sophomore year of college, when she had the opportunity to visit the racing country of Kentucky. From Churchill Downs to Old Friends Thoroughbred Retirement Facility, it was the trip of a lifetime. But no moment stands out to her like meeting Cigar, arguably world's greatest racehorse until his death this Fall. Upon meeting Man o' War, Walter Farley wrote, "Man o' War stood in the doorway, statuesque and magnificent. There was a lordly life to his head and his sharp eyes were bright. He didn't look at us, but far over our heads...I was aware of only one thing—that for the first and perhaps only time in my life, I was in the presence of a horse that was truly great, and it would be a moment always to be remembered." This was what Jordan felt on meeting Cigar. And this is what she hopes to convey in her poem.

———————

Marcella Cross is 14 years-old and lives on a small sheep farm in Oregon, she love to write poems and read books. Her sister is Emily Cross and they wrote their poems together. (Winner Honorable Mention)

Marilyn Burkhardt is an artist and writer from the Oregon Coast. Her rescued draft horses (mother & daughter Rachel & Jewell) roamed her property for ten years. They now lie side-by-side under the apple tree.

Nina E. Larsen has published work in Norway, the UK, Ireland, the U.S., and was chosen by esteemed poet, Billy Collins, for an Honorary Mention in the 2012 Fish Poetry Prize.

Clare Mazur is a member of the Meetinghouse Poets of Glastonbury,

Connecticut and the first place recipient of the 2014 Gerard F. Melito Senior Poetry Contest.

Phyllis Price, a Virginia native, is a writer and photographer using images and words to express the relationship of nature and man.

Jacqueline Kolosov's Half-Andalusian mare inspired her poem. Her third collection of poetry is *Memory Of Blue*.

Joan Leotta is an author, journalist, poet and story performer who has loved horses all of her life and still dreams of visiting Kentucky.

Rebecca Baez is a wife, mother, and grandmother who breeds and loves Andalusian horses.

Mary Wlodarski lives with her family and two horses in Minnesota where she is working on her manuscript titled *Speak Horse*.

Matt Kraunelis is a Massachusetts based poet. His chapbook *Tackle Box* is available from Finishing Line Press.

Kathy Truders enjoys her passion for horses at her farm in rural Platte County, Missouri, where her heart is owned by three Percheron mares and memories of Duke.

Jerri Hardesty lives in the woods of Alabama with husband, Kirk, also a poet. Jerri has had approximately 325 poems published, won more than 600 awards and titles in both written and spoken word/performance poetry.

Hélène Cardona is a poet, actor, and equestrian, whose latest books are *Dreaming My Animal Selves, Life in Suspension,* and *Beyond Elsewhere.*

DeMar Regier cherishes nature, a wellspring for the poetry, gift books and children's stories she writes from her home in Prairie Village, Kansas.

Gwen Hart teaches writing at Buena Vista University in Storm Lake, Iowa.

Jim LaVilla-Havelin is the author of four books of poetry, *Counting* is the most recent. He is the San Antonio Coordinator of National Poetry Month and the Poetry Editor of the *San Antonio Express-News*.

Miriam Bat-Ami is a horse lover and author of children's, YA, and adult works. She has leased, owned, taught, and learned from these beautiful creatures.

Lisa Underwood, a freelance writer with a M.A. in Journalism from the University of North Carolina at Chapel Hill, lives in Greensboro with one husband, two sons, four dogs, two cats and a chinchilla.

Mary McDonough, Ph.D is an ethicist who writes on various topics such as religion, music, health care, animals and is a devout equestrian!

Patricia Brooks is the published author of two novels, and short fiction and poetry in a variety of journals. She is also the grandmother of Marcella and Emily Cross, winners of the two Honorable Mention!

Barbara MacKay participates in writing groups and poetry readings in Mendocino County in California.

Emily Cross is 16 years-old, she lives with her family on a sheep farm. In her spare time she loves to read, write, tend to her honeybees and bind books. By binding books, she makes book covers out of cardboard and scrapbooking papers and then she make pages out of printer paper. She folds the paper into signatures, which are groups of papers, and then she uses embroidery thread to bind the pages and covers together. She uses these to write in most often. Her poem was inspired by a series by John Flanagan, an Australian author, called *Ranger's Apprentice*, and the main character is often talking to his horse. It is one of her favorite book series. Her sister is Marcella Cross and they are winners of the two Honorable Mentions.

Leah Maines has edited over 800 poetry, fiction, and play collections, including several award-winning titles. She is the publisher of Finishing Line Press. She is former Poet-in-Residence of Northern Kentucky

University (funded in part by the Kentucky Humanities Council and the National Endowment for the Humanities). She is the author of two poetry books. Her first book was nominated for the Pushcart Prize and the Williams Carlos Williams Book Award (Poetry Society of America). *Looking to the East with Western Eyes, New Women's Voices Series, No. 1* (Finishing Line Press, 1998) reached #10 in the « Cincinnati/Tri-State Best Sellers List » (Cincinnati Enquirer), and is now in its fourth printing. Her most recent collection, *Beyond the River*, (KWC Press, 2002, 1st edition) won the Kentucky Writers' Coalition Poetry Chapbook Competition in 2002. Her poems have appeared in numerous national and international publications including *Nebo, Owen Wister Review, Licking River Review, Flyway* and other literary magazines and anthologies. Leah lived in Gifu, Japan where she studied and researched classical Japanese poetry at Gifu University. She also studied at Kings College London, England, and The Marino Institute in Dublin, Ireland. She holds degrees from Cincinnati Christian University and Northern Kentucky University.

———————

CPSIA information can be obtained
at www.ICGtesting.com
Printed in the USA
LVOW04s1047291215

468215LV00001B/10/P

9 781622 299164